Bella BEADED *Jewelry*

Artful Italian Designs with Wire, Thread, Cord & Ribbon

Donatella Ciotti

SOMERSET CO. LIBRARY
BRIDGEWATER, N.J. 08807

INTERWEAVE PRESS

W9-CON-312

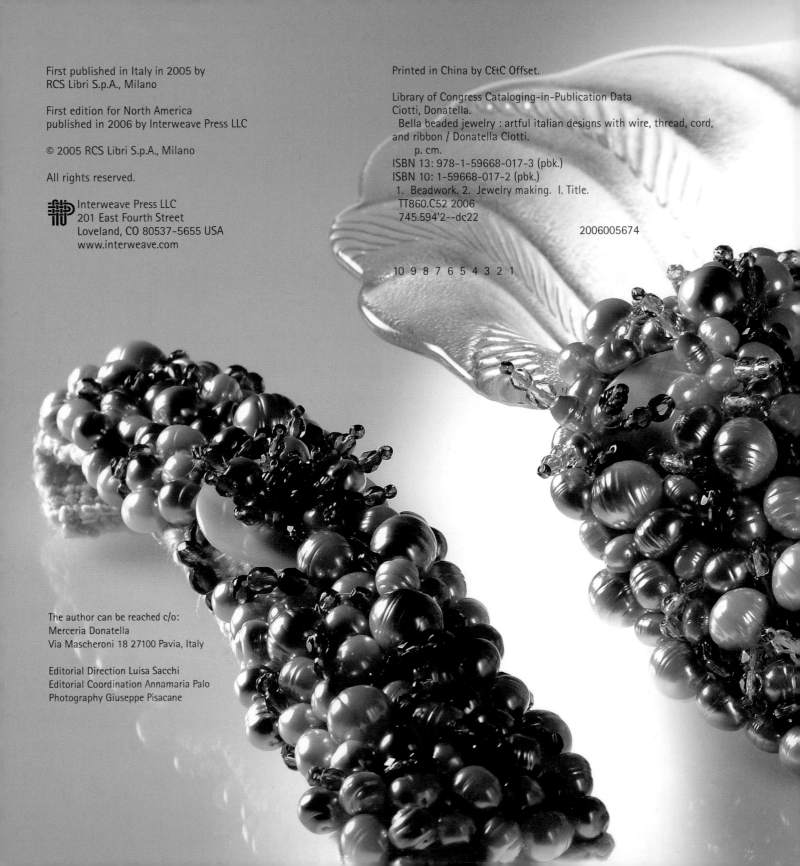

First published in Italy in 2005 by
RCS Libri S.p.A., Milano

First edition for North America
published in 2006 by Interweave Press LLC

© 2005 RCS Libri S.p.A., Milano

All rights reserved.

Interweave Press LLC
201 East Fourth Street
Loveland, CO 80537-5655 USA
www.interweave.com

Printed in China by C&C Offset.

Library of Congress Cataloging-in-Publication Data
Ciotti, Donatella.
  Bella beaded jewelry : artful italian designs with wire, thread, cord,
and ribbon / Donatella Ciotti.
    p. cm.
ISBN 13: 978-1-59668-017-3 (pbk.)
ISBN 10: 1-59668-017-2 (pbk.)
 1. Beadwork. 2. Jewelry making. I. Title.
TT860.C52 2006
745.594'2--dc22

                          2006005674

10 9 8 7 6 5 4 3 2 1

The author can be reached c/o:
Merceria Donatella
Via Mascheroni 18 27100 Pavia, Italy

Editorial Direction Luisa Sacchi
Editorial Coordination Annamaria Palo
Photography Giuseppe Pisacane

CONTENTS

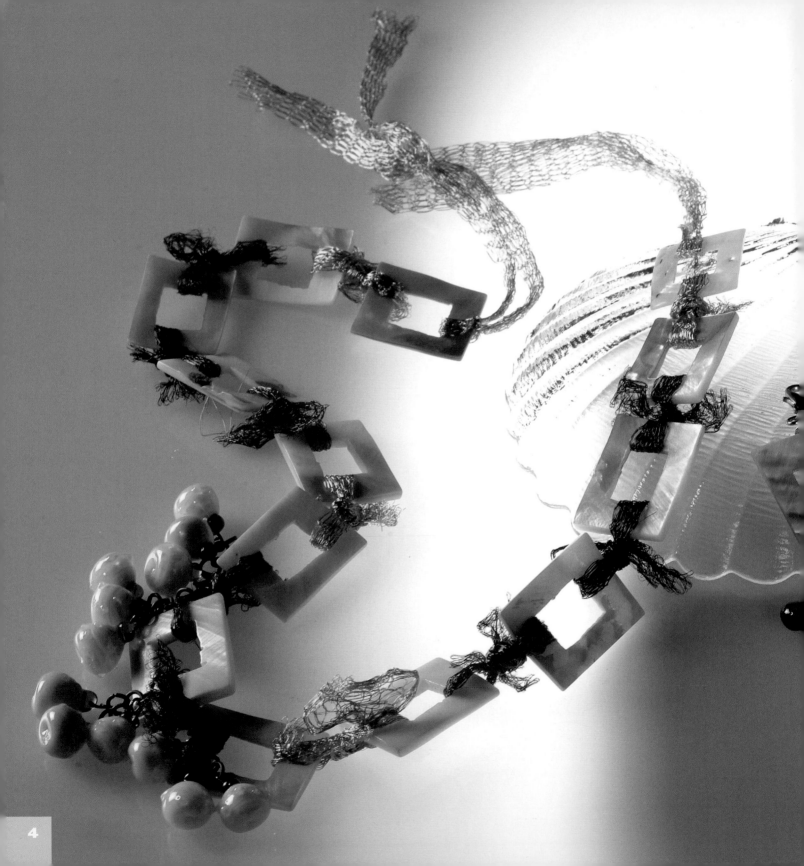

Introduction

What will be in style next season? Which colors will be fashionable? In *Bella Beaded Jewelry* you'll find exciting ideas that reflect emerging international fashion trends, reflected in innovative materials and techniques.

Even the most cutting-edge fashion is inspired by styles from the past while it looks to the future. That's why you will find hints of the bijoux of the 1960s and 1970s here, including mother-of-pearl, chains, glass fruit, colored woods, and translucent drops that hang from simple cords or chains. These projects include a nod to the latest trend:

vintage costume jewelry, brought to life here with myriad beads and baroque pearls of soft, iridescent colors reminiscent of the ocean floor.

And we can't forget the classic, elegant jewelry made with a crochet hook or filigreed mesh, accompanied by delightful bracelets with jingling dangles. Among the new ideas are very light good luck charms, for moments to be lived to the fullest.

There is sure to be something to please everyone in the artful Italian designs found in the pages ahead!

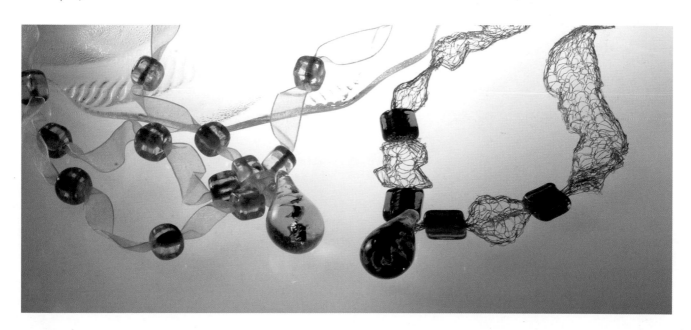

Pearls, Beads, and Crystals

1 Venetian glass
2 Venetian drop with gold vein
3 Millefiori beads
4 Freshwater pearls
5 Glass fruit, vegetables, and candy
6 Mother-of-pearl figures
7 Colored mother-of-pearl buttons in various shapes
8 Crystals
9 Glass beads
10 Syrian glass in various shapes
11 Wooden beads

Tools, Supplies, and Findings

1 Round-nose pliers
2 Wire cutters
3 Flat-nose pliers
4 Silver wire
5 Epoxy
6 Beading needles
7 Screen finding for bracelet
8 Chain mail neckpiece
9 Screen finding for charm
10 Cabochon
11 Screen finding for clasp
12 Screen finding for earring
13 Lobster clasps
14 Barrel clasps
15 Flexible wire
16 Filigree charm
17 Floral filigree earrings
18 Large-link centerpiece
   for necklaces
19 Memory wire
20 French ear wires
21 Crimp beads
22 Safety pins and head pins
23 Fold-over cord ends
24 Knot cups
25 11-hole clasp
26 Separator bars
27 Jump rings

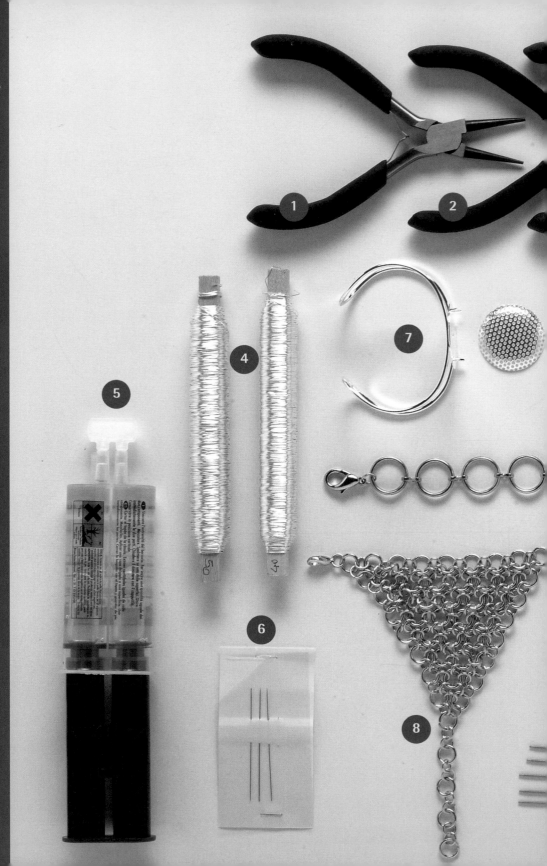

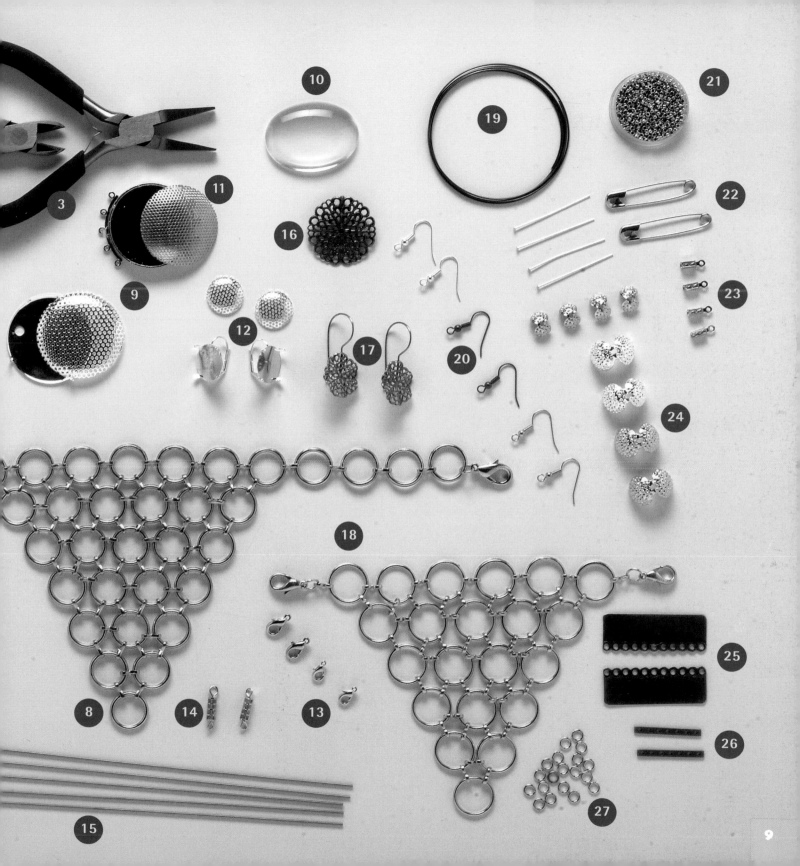

Stringing Materials

1 Silk cord
2 Waxed cord in different
  colors and sizes
3 Metallic tubular mesh ribbon
4 Naturally colored cord
5 Beading wire

Basic Techniques

Surgeon's Knot

Step 1. When the piece is finished the threads are joined with a double knot in which the threads pass through the second loop twice. Carefully pull the thread ends.

Simple Loop

Step 1. String the first bead onto the head pin and slide it to the end. With the round-nose pliers, starting from the top of the last bead, gently bend the wire at a 90° angle about ¼" (.63 cm) from the bead.

Step 2. Wrap the wire around the tip of the round-nose pliers and gently shape it into a simple loop.

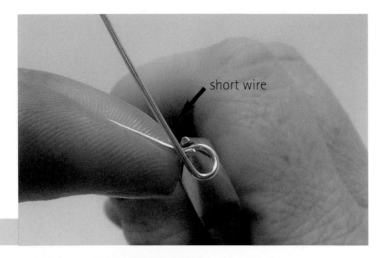

Wrapped Loop

Step 1. Cut a piece of 22-gauge wire about 12"
(30.5cm) long. Mark the wire 1½" (3.8cm) from
the end. Mark the round-nose pliers about ¼"
(.63 mm) from the tip of jaws.

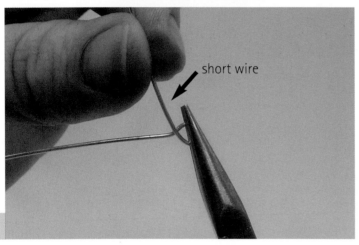

Step 2. Place wire in pliers and line up the mark on
the wire with the mark on the pliers. Make a loop
by bending the short wire around the pliers, then
up. Keep rotating your hand until the short end
of the wire is facing straight up and the long end
is on the left side.

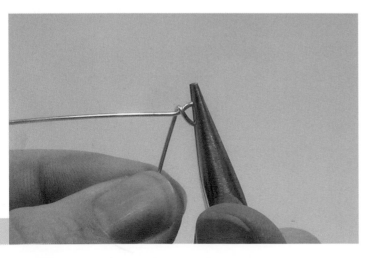

Step 3. Use needle-nose pliers to grip the loop.
Bend the loop up slightly to create an angle on
the long-wire side of the loop. Place the needle-
nose pliers across half the loop to support it
while you begin to wrap.

short wire

short wire

Step 4. Begin wrapping by bringing the short wire to the back of the long wire and then down. Bring the short wire up and keep wrapping until you have two or three wraps.

Step 5. Cut off the rest of the short wire after you are finished wrapping, remembering that the flat side of the cutters should face the wire. Press the cut wire in place with needle-nose pliers.

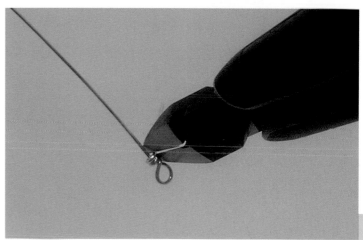

Step 6. It may be necessary to use the needle-nose pliers to squeeze the wraps together, squeezing toward the loop. If needed, you can use round-nose pliers to re-round the loop.

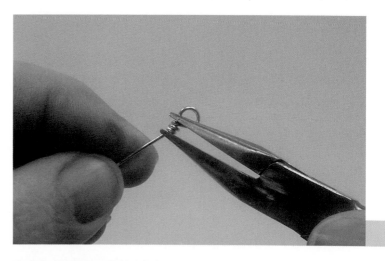

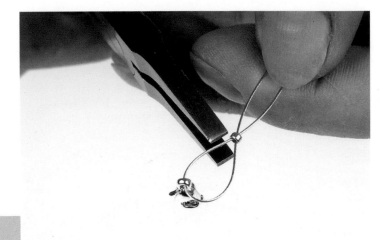

Crimp Beads
Step 1. To attach a clasp to beading wire, insert the crimp bead onto the wire, pass the thread through the hole of the clasp, pass it back through the crimp bead, and flatten the crimp bead with the flat-nose pliers.

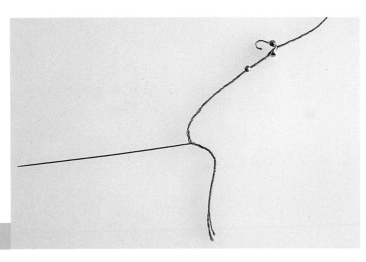

Knot Cup
Step 1. To finish a string of beads with a knot cup, pass the thread end through the hole in the cup.

Step 2. Put a crimp bead on the thread, pushing it to the center of the cup. With the flat-nose pliers, squeeze it so that the thread cannot slide. Cut the excess thread. With the pliers, close the caps of the cup so that the thread ends up well-anchored inside.

To End Two Wires or Threads With a Knot Cup

Step 1. At the end of a necklace or bracelet, thread a knot cup and pass the two wires or threads through the hole of the cup. Then make two very tight knots.

Step 2. Cut the excess wire or thread, put a drop of glue on the knot, then close the cup with flat-nose pliers.

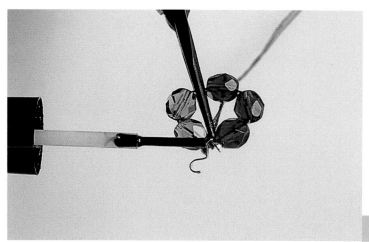

Fold-over Cord End

Step 1. Insert the cord in the fold-over cord end and, with the flat-nose pliers, bend the two sides one at a time, making them meet at the center.

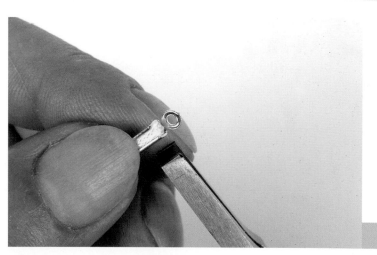

Cord Wrap

Step 1. To make this finish, use a piece of cord of a greater diameter than the one used for your work. On the ends of the work, place the piece of cord forming a very large loop. Holding it still on the base cords, work with one end, leaving the other one free.

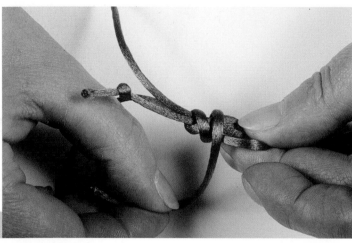

Step 2. Wrap it several times around the threads that you are joining: every wrapping has the double goal of making the knot bigger and more secure. Make the wraps tight and close together to keep the wrap from coming undone.

Step 3. To finish it, slip the winding cord into the part of the loop left free by the spirals and then pull the two cord ends simultaneously. With smooth, quick execution, this knot can add subtle beauty and volume that makes it particularly decorative and suitable for closing ethnic-style necklaces.

Twisting Wire

Step 1. If you used metal wire to finish the work, twist the two ends of the wire around themselves two or three times. Cut the excess and hide the intertwining junction.

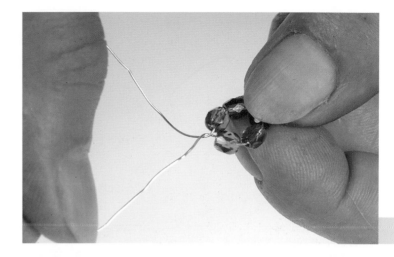

Coil

Step 1. To create a flat coil for closing, make the first turn with the round-nose pliers forming a small circle. Continue winding it around itself forming a spiral, keeping it flat.

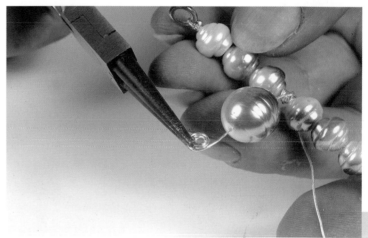

Jump ring

Step 1. To open jump rings use two sets of pliers. Always open them in an S form, so that they can close perfectly again.

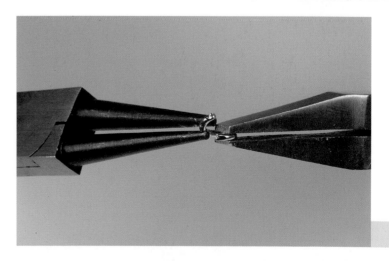

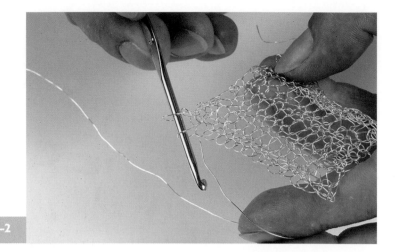

Crochet Stitch

Step 1. Make a basic chain of desired size.

Step 2. Insert the hook in the center of the next stitch and pull up a loop.

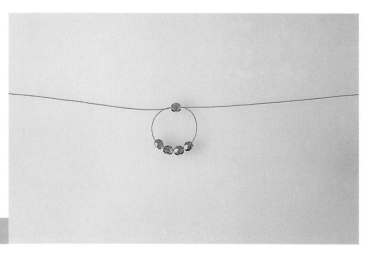

Step 3. Bring the wire over the hook again and pull it through both loops on the hook. One loop remains on the hook. Repeat Steps 2 and 3 until reaching your desired length and width.

Ladder Stitch

Step 1. This type of work is for rings, pendants, and bracelets. String the beads and run them to the center of the thread on which you are working. Continue by crossing the two ends of the thread through the inside of a bead. Use a nylon thread size D or beading wire.

Ending a Multistrand Piece

Step 1. To tie a group of cords (at the end of a work), bind them with a piece of wire that you will close by twisting the two ends together.

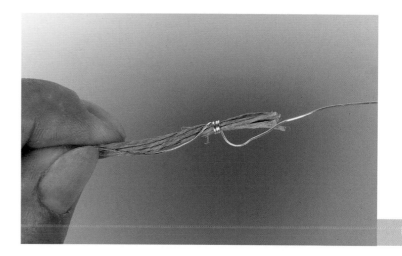

Step 2. Pass a head pin under the binding, form a loop, and secure it at the top part of the binding.

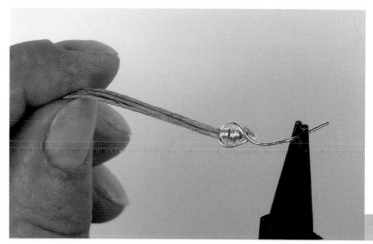

Step 3. Insert the knot cup on the excess part of the head pin, bring it near the binding, and close it. Insert the lobster clasp, and with the round-nose pliers, create a simple loop.

Pearls and Mother-of-Pearl

Precious Choker

Materials

- 1 screen mesh clasp
- 20 grams size 11° seed beads
- 180 pink pearls of various sizes
  (shown here 6, 8, 10, and 12mm)
- 118" (300cm) length complementary 20-gauge wire
- 8 crimp beads
- 314" (798cm) length
  single-thread nylon thread

Tools

- Wire cutters
- Flat-nose pliers
- Size 10 beading needle

Step 1. For the centerpiece, take the screen mesh clasp, cut a piece of nylon thread, pass one end through the mesh, insert a crimp bead, and squeeze it with the flat-nose pliers (see page 16). Pass the other end of the thread (without the crimp bead) to the right side through the central hole. Thread 4 pearls and a seed bead, pass the thread back through the 4 pearls and back through the hole in the screen. Pull the thread firmly.

Step 2. Continue adding stacks of pearls topped with a seed bead, until the mesh is filled. Then position the mesh in the setting and with the flat-nose pliers, squeeze the 4 prongs to secure. Put a small piece of cardboard between the pliers and the clasp to avoid leaving marks.

Step 3. Attach a length of beading wire to an eye on one side of the clasp with a crimp bead (see page 16). String pearls and beads on the beading wire to your desired length. Fasten to the corresponding eye on the other side of the clasp with a crimp bead. Repeat for each set of eyes on your clasp.

Crocheted Necklace and Bracelet

Materials for the Necklace
- Wire or sport-weight cotton yarn for crochet base
- Assorted pearls of your choice, based on the size of the center-piece (shown here 90 pearls sizes 6, 8, 10, and 12mm)
- Mother-of-pearl figure for center-piece (shown here 3cm × 2cm)
- 1 bobbin polyester sewing thread
- Size 10 beading needle
- 100–120 crystals no larger than 5mm
- 20 grams of two colors size 11° seed beads to coordinate with the pearls and crystals
- 39" (99cm) length of ½" (1.27cm) wide pink organza ribbon

Tools for the Necklace
- Scissors
- Nylon sewing thread
- Size 3 crochet hook

Tools for the Bracelet
- Scissors

Materials for the Bracelet
- About 80 pearls 6, 8, 10, and 12mm
- Mother-of-pearl figure for center-piece (shown here 3cm × 2cm)
- 1 bobbin of polyester sewing thread
- Size 10 beading needle
- 50–60 crystals no larger than 4mm
- 20 grams size 11° seed beads
- 4" (10cm) length of Velcro

Step 1. After making the crochet-stitched base, (see p. 20) in the size and shape desired, begin the beadwork from the center of the piece. Position a mother-of-pearl figure and, on the thread coming out of the hole from this piece, string a pearl, 2 crystals, and a small bead. Pass the thread back through the 2 crystals, the pearl, and in the hole of the mother-of-pearl piece, and return to the other side.

Step 2. Repeat the same thing on the other hole. Continue stringing pearls and crystals. Begin sewing the pearls, and continue filling the empty spaces with loops and clusters of crystal, as you did in Step 1. Create a harmonious piece alternating large and small pearls, with nuances in color. Cut the organza ribbon in half and sew a piece to each side of the base.

Step 3. To make the bracelet, follow the preceding directions. For the clasp, sew a piece of Velcro to each end.

Note: An alternative to the crochet base is to use a piece of Ultrasuede or leather.

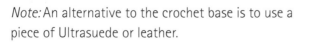

Mother-of-Pearl Collar and Bracelet

Materials for the Collar

- 10 mother-of-pearl 3cm rounds
- 7 mother-of-pearl 5cm × 4cm rhombuses
- 8 pink 12mm pearls
- 1 large-loop chain-mail neckpiece
- 157" (399cm) of 18-gauge silver wire
- 39" (99cm) length of gold organza ribbon ½" (1cm) wide

Materials for the Bracelet

- 80 pearls of various sizes
- 20" (50cm) length of complementary beading wire
- 354" (899cm) length of 20-gauge silver wire
- 1 lobster clasp
- 1 soldered ring
- 2 crimp beads

Tools for the Collar and Bracelet

- Round-nose pliers
- Wire cutters

Step 1. Cut a 4" (10cm) length of silver wire, and pass it through the hole of the mother-of-pearl. Wrap one end around the other for several turns and trim the end neatly. Pass the remaining end through the ring of the collar and wrap it above the previous wrap. Work on the whole center-piece in this manner. Turn the end of a piece of wire on the end of your round-nose pliers and make a simple loop (see page 13).

Step 2. String a pearl, pass it through a ring, and make a wrapped loop (see page 14). Work both sides of the chain in this manner. Divide the organza in half, insert the piece of organza in the last ring, and make a knot to secure it. Repeat on the other side.

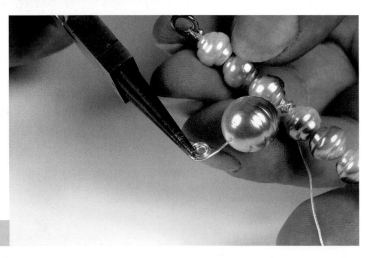

For the bracelet, take the piece of beading wire and string the pearls until you reach your desired length. Put the lobster clasp on one end, and the small ring on the other end. Cut a 4" (10cm) length of silver wire and make a tight wrapped loop between two pearls (see page 14). Trim the wrapped end. String a pearl on the other end of the wire and create a coil with the round-nose pliers (see page 19).

SMALL-LINK CENTERPIECE VARIATION
This piece is constructed with pearl bead
dangles made with silver wire. The necklace is strung with beading wire.

Pearl Waterfall

Materials
- 3 mother-of-pearl 5cm rings
- 50 pink 12mm pearls
- 80 oval 6mm pearls
- About 180 4mm crystals
- Size 11° seed beads to match the crystals
- 2 large knot cups
- 2 head pins
- 1 lobster clasp
- 1 soldered ring
- Crimp beads
- 10' (3m) of complementary beading wire

Tools
- Flat-nose pliers
- Wire cutters

Step 1. To make the loops on the mother-of-pearl ring, take a piece of beading wire, string a crimp bead, some crystals, and some pearls, and pass it through the center of the mother-of-pearl ring. Pass the same piece of wire back through the crimp bead and pull it tightly. Squeeze the crimp bead with the flat-nose pliers (see page 16). Trim the short end of the beading wire neatly.

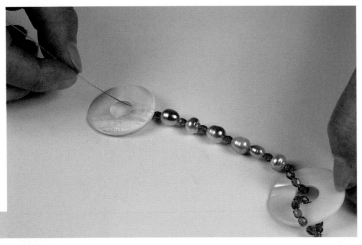

Step 2. On the other end of the wire, string pearls and crystals to your desired length. Create a new loop in the second mother-of-pearl ring. For pendants, create a loop around the mother-of-pearl ring for the necklace, string pearls and crystals, and then string a crimp bead and squeeze it so that it secures your work. Trim the excess wire.

Step 3. For the clasp of the necklace, make small loops in the ends of the beading wires with crimp beads. Pass a head pin through the loops to gather them, and make a simple loop with the round-nose pliers to secure them together (see page 13). Pass the head pin through the opening of a large knot cup. Close the knot cup to hide the loops of beading wire gathered on the head pin (see page 16). Thread a lobster clasp on the head pin and, with your round-nose pliers, make a wrapped loop to secure it (see page 14). Repeat this step on the other side, using a soldered ring instead of the lobster clasp.

PEARL WATERFALL VARIATION
This variation is made with rows of
seed beads alternating with Venetian
glass, and mother-of-pearl pieces
hooked between them. To make the
necklace more precious you can make
multiple strands of pearls that end
with mother-of-pearl.

Interwoven Mother-of-Pearl

Materials for the Necklace
- 13 mother-of-pearl
  4cm × 2.5cm buckles
- 12 glass 10mm lemon beads
- 36 jump rings
- 39" (99cm) length each of metallic
  tubular mesh ribbons in various
  colors (1/2" [1.3cm] wide)

Tools for the Necklace
- Scissors
- Round-nose pliers

Materials for the Bracelet
- 4 mother-of-pearl
  4cm × 2.5cm buckles
- 8 glass 8mm tomato beads
- 8 glass 2cm mushroom beads
- 79" (201cm) length of
  20-gauge silver wire
- 1 lobster clasp
- 1 jump ring

Tools for the Bracelet
- Wire cutters
- Round-nose pliers

Step 1. For the necklace, cut 8" (20cm) of metallic tubular mesh ribbon, thread 2 buckles, and tie the ribbon with a surgeon's knot (see page 13), then fan the ends of the ribbon out. Continue in this manner, connecting the buckles and alternating the colors of the ribbon. Then create playful dangles in the center. Put the glass lemons together with jump rings, in groups of three. Hook the groups of lemons to the knotted ribbons with another jump ring.

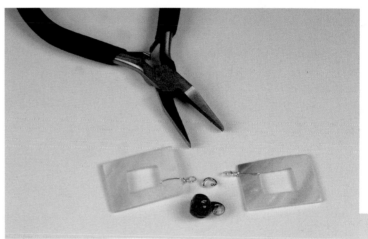

Step 2. Wrap a 6" (15cm) piece of silver wire on one side of a buckle. Twist one end twice around and trim the excess. On the other end create a loop and make two twists on top of the previous ones. Trim the excess. Repeat on the other side of the buckle. Connect the buckles with rings. Connect a jump ring to each glass vegetable. Connect each group of 4 vegetables with another jump ring, and attach the groups of vegetables to the buckle connections.

Egyptian Collar

Materials
- 36 safety pins
- 195 gray 8mm pearls
- 7 gray 12mm pearls
- 79" (201cm) length of complementary thread
- 4 crimp beads
- 1 lobster clasp
- 1 soldered ring
- 10 small soldered rings
- 197" (500cm) length of silver beading wire

Tools
- Round-nose pliers
- Wire cutters

Step 1. Preparation of the pins: Open 18 safety pins and put 3 pearls on each. Close them and, with flat-nose pliers, lightly squeeze the head to keep them from coming unhooked. Then cut 2 pieces of beading wire, 1 of 24" (60cm) and 1 of 36" (90cm). Thread 5 pearls on one, and 6 on the other. Then start stringing on the pins, one empty and one with the pearls, alternating with the pearls.

Step 2. On the outer, larger curve, you will need to augment the number of pearls in a way that gives roundness to the collar. During this step, insert some soldered rings in the central part of the outer curve between the pearls. You will attach the dangles on these.

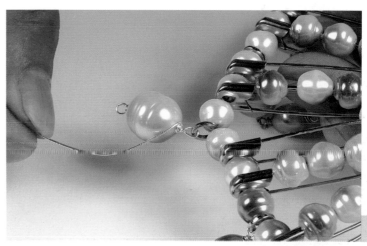

Step 3. For the dangles: Take a piece of 4" (10cm) silver wire, and with the round-nose pliers create a small wrapped loop on the end of the wire (see page 14). Trim the loop. String a pearl on the remaining end and create a new wrapped loop. Hook groups of pearls together, inserting the wire of each pearl in the loop of a preceding pearl.

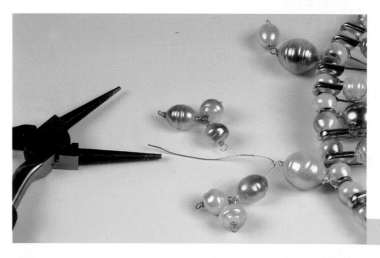

Glass,
Silk Thread,
and Cord

Teardrop

Materials
- 18 small flowers in Syrian glass
- 1 glass 8cm (length) drop pendant
- 2 glass 4cm × 1.5cm rectangles
- 236" (600cm) length of red cord
- 236" (600cm) length of loden green cord
- 2 large knot cups
- 1 lobster clasp
- 1 small soldered ring
- 2 head pins

Tools
- Scissors
- Wire cutters
- Round-nose pliers

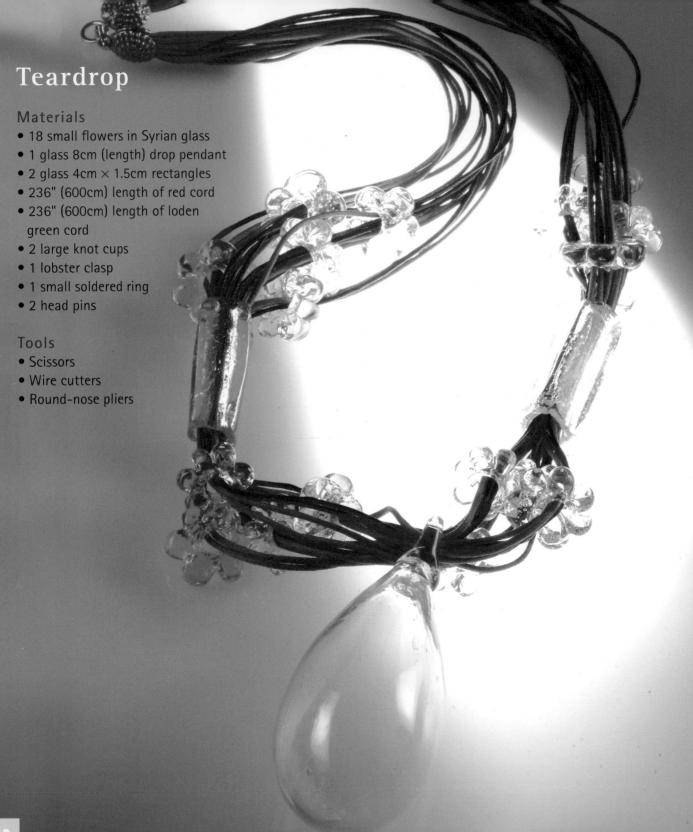

Step 1. Cut the cord into 24" (60cm) pieces, pass all of them through the eyelet of the drop, and bring the drop to the center. Do the following on both sides: Divide the cords into four groups and on each slide 1 glass flower. Then pass all of the cords through the hole of one of the rectangular pieces.

Step 2. After making the first cluster, create a second. Divide the cords into five groups and on each slide 1 flower. Even the cords, and bind them together with a piece of wire. Pass a head pin under the binding and create a loop.

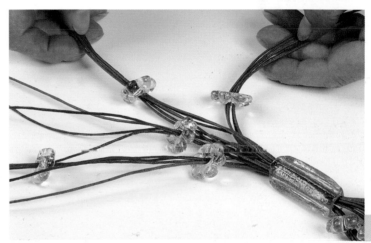

Step 3. Pass the head pin through the hole in the knot cup in a way that covers the binding (see page 16). Position the lobster clasp and make a wrapped loop (see page 14). Repeat on the other side, where you'll put a soldered ring instead.

Colors of
the Sun

Materials
- 1 skein of orange Seta Mare silk thread
- 1 glass 4cm × 1.50cm rectangular bead
- 1 glass 4cm × 2.50cm barrel bead
- 1 glass 3cm × 2cm barrel bead

Tools
- Scissors

Step 1. Open the skein and cut it in half on only one side in such a way that you have threads about 71" (180cm) in length. Insert the rectangular glass piece on one side of the skein, then cross the other part, inserting it through the glass in the opposite direction.

Step 2. Continue the work by inserting a new large glass barrel piece on one side and cross again, inserting the other part in the opposite direction. Finish with a small barrel piece and on this, cross the two ends of the skein. When you have strung all of the glass in this manner, pull the threads tightly.

Step 3. After finishing the neckpiece, make a knot with all of the free threads. Even the threads and cut them, leaving the desired length to form a tassel.

Colors of
the Forest

Materials

- 1 skein of Seta Mare gray silk (50g/2oz)
- 10 amber 2cm × 2cm triangle beads
- 2 amber 4cm flower beads
- 4 amber 3cm disk beads

Tools

- Scissors

Step 1. Open the skein, unwind it, and stretch it well to release any kinky folds. Cut it only on one side. Take about 30 threads from the skein and double them. On the big skein, in the center, make a knot through the center of which you will pass the threads you have just doubled. Tighten the knot in a way that it secures the small skein, which will serve as a pendant.

Step 2. To finish the piece, bend a piece of wire to create a kind of needle with an eye. Insert some of the silk threads through the eye of your improvised needle and pass them through the hole of the bead. Repeat until all threads are pulled through the bead.

Step 3. Secure the bead with a knot. Repeat these steps to finish both the necklace and the small tassel.

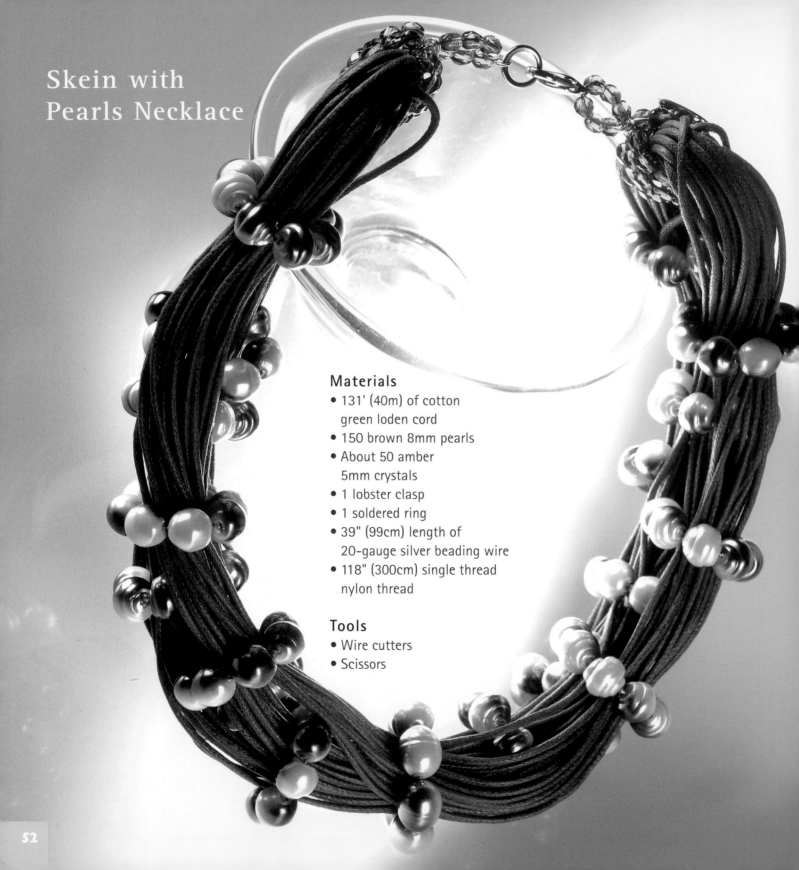

Skein with Pearls Necklace

Materials
- 131' (40m) of cotton green loden cord
- 150 brown 8mm pearls
- About 50 amber 5mm crystals
- 1 lobster clasp
- 1 soldered ring
- 39" (99cm) length of 20-gauge silver beading wire
- 118" (300cm) single thread nylon thread

Tools
- Wire cutters
- Scissors

Step 1. With the cord make a skein of 16" (40cm) without cutting the two ends, and tie with 12" (30cm) of beading wire. String the pearls on a piece of nylon thread, wind it up on part of the cords from the skein and join the ends by tying a surgeon's knot (see page 13). Start from the center.

Step 2. Continue working in this manner, creating new rings. Each time choose a group of cords from the skein not gathered in the preceding ring.

Step 3. String the crystals on a piece of silver wire and wrap them around the end of the skein in such a way that they cover the preceding binding, made with metal wire (see Step 1). At the end of the third wrap string 4 crystals, 1 lobster clasp, and 4 crystals, and twist in a way that creates a loop. Repeat on the other side, inserting a soldered ring.

Basket Weave
Necklace

Materials
• 70 millefiori 1cm glass beads
• 155' (47m) of blue cotton cord
• 315" (800cm) of 18-gauge silver wire

Tools
• Wire cutters
• Round-nose pliers
• Scissors

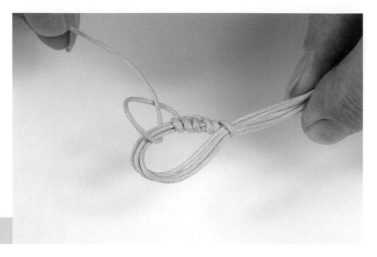

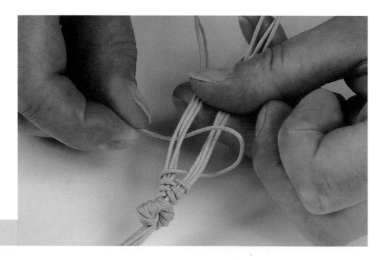

Step 1. For the first side of the necklace, cut 10 pieces of cord 59" (150cm) long and one piece 9 yd (8m) long. Tie them together on one side and double them. Take the longer end and make a knot around the bunch of cords. Using the cord with which you made the knot, work the loop to make half hitches around the loop. The cord passes through the loop from high to low and goes out of the center of the loop that has been formed.

Step 2. Pull the cord tightly. For the other side of the necklace, cut 20 pieces of 2½' (75cm) cord and a 315" (800cm) piece. Tie them on one side and make a knot. This will serve as a clasp to insert in the eyelet.

Step 3. Begin the basket weaving. Divide the bunch into two equal parts. The longer cord (of 315" [800cm]) will pass from above to below in one direction, from above to below in the opposite direction. Continue in this way for 50 crossings.

Step 4. Cut a 4" (10cm) length of silver beading wire, with the round-nose pliers make a small wrapped loop (see page 14), and at the base of this wrap the shorter end two or three times. Trim the short end neatly. Then string a millefiori bead on the wire and make a wrapped loop on the other side with your round-nose pliers. Trim the excess wire.

Step 5. In this manner, prepare 10 dangles with individual millefiori beads and 10 dangles with 2 millefiori beads linked together. After making about 50 winding crossings, begin positioning the millefiori dangles with the cord. String them on the group of outer cords and space them with 2 or 3 basket windings.

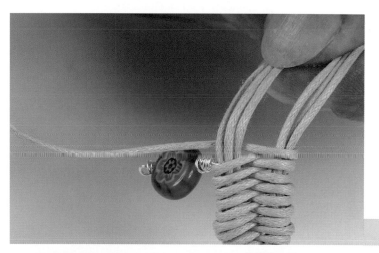

Step 6. After working on both sides of the necklace in the way described above, regroup all of the cords and make a knot to keep them all together. Cut the cords of the tassel to the desired length. String a dangle on one of the cords, and secure it with a knot. Repeat several more times.

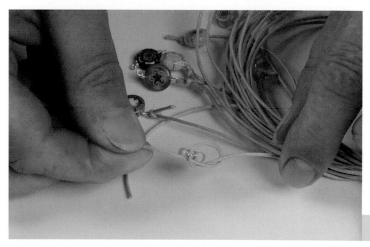

Hot Peppers!

Materials
- 10 glass 3.5cm
  hot pepper beads
- 8 glass 2cm
  yellow pepper beads
- 8 glass 2cm
  red pepper beads
- 80 pieces of flexible wire
- 132' (40m) of red
  waxed cord

Tools
- Scissors

Step 1. Cut 19 pieces of waxed cord 6½' (2m) long each and one 8½' (2.5m) long. Even them, double them, and make a loop. With all the cords, make a knot at the base of the loop, then a second at 16–18" (40–50cm) from the first, according to the desired length of your necklace. This will be the base of the necklace on which you'll work. Use the end of the longer cord to make half hitches around the loop as on page 56. Hide the end of the cord in the large knot.

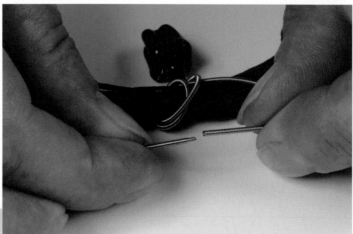

Step 2. Take a piece of flexible wire, pass it through the hole of a vegetable bead, roll it up toward the gathered cords, and create a first knot. Roll the wire a second time toward the gathered cords and make another knot. Repeat the whole operation, but instead of the knot this time fasten the ends of the wire together.

Step 3. Repeat Step 2 twice, but without the bead.

Step 4. Repeat Steps 2 and 3 until all the wire pieces and vegetable beads have been used.

COLORED BRACELETS AND EARRINGS
This variation was made with jump rings,
chain, and glass vegetable beads.

Fruit Salad

Materials for the Ring
- 1 screen mesh ring finding
- 197" (500cm) length of
  18-gauge silver wire
- 25 glass 1cm cherry beads
- 10 glass 1cm leaf beads
- 40 transparent 5mm crystals
- 40 head pins

Tools for the Ring
- Wire cutters
- Round-nose pliers

Materials for the Earrings
- 12 glass 3.5cm yellow
  pepper beads
- 18 glass 2cm yellow
  leaf beads
- 58" (147cm) length
  of 20-gauge silver beading wire
- 2 lobster clasps

Tools for the Earrings
- Wire cutters

Rings

Step 1. Insert a head pin through the center hole of the mesh, string a crystal, cut a small part from the head pin, and with the help of the round-nose pliers create a wrapped loop (see page 14). Continue in this manner until you have filled the mesh. Cut a piece of silver wire, insert it in the loop of one of the cherry beads, and make a wrapped loop.

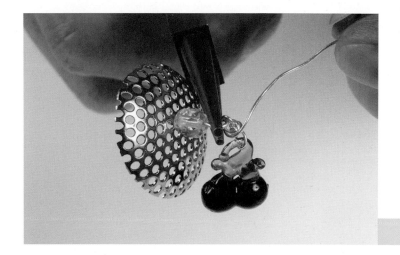

Step 2. Trim the excess wire. Prepare all of the cherry and leaf beads in this manner. Pass the remaining end of the wire on one of the cherry beads through one of the loops created on the base in Step 1. Trim the excess. Repeat until all the cherry and leaf beads have been attached.

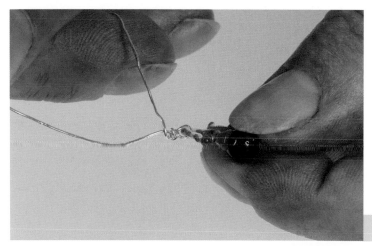

Earrings

Step 1. Cut 2 lengths of 10" (25cm) silver wire. Twist part of them, string a glass piece on one of the wires, and twist again. Continue to string glass beads as you like, continuing to twist the wires. When you have finished the composition, close the two ends with a small wrapped loop and connect to the loop of an ear wire.

Wires

Caged Pearls

Materials
- 5 mother-of-pearl 4cm flowers
- 3 Venetian glass 2cm × 1cm flower-shaped beads
- 2 Venetian glass 2.5cm × 1.5cm leaf-shaped beads
- 5 Venetian glass 2.5cm × 1.5cm rectangular beads
- 4 Venetian glass 1cm cubes
- 15 jump rings
- 315" (800cm) length of 20-gauge silver wire
- 1 lobster clasp
- 1 soldered ring

Tools
- Round-nose pliers
- Wire cutters

Step 1. Cut a 4" (10cm) length of silver beading wire, and insert it in the hole of a flower. Use round-nose pliers to make a wrapped loop with 2 wraps (see page 14). Trim the excess. Use round-nose pliers to make 2 wraps with the other end of the wire, directly over the previously made wraps.

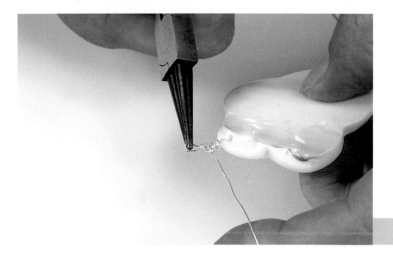

Step 2. Cut a 27" (70cm) length of silver beading wire. Hold the starting end on one side of the flower and with the other end make 4–5 wraps around it. Finish on the opposite side from the start.

Step 3. With the round-nose pliers make a wrapped loop (see page 14) with each end of the wire that will serve as a hook between the mother-of-pearl pieces. Work the wires of the caging around the mother-of-pearl with the pliers, creating whatever motifs you like. Proceed in the same way with the Venetian glass. Wrap the Venetian glass rectangular beads in a like manner. Make dangles from the other Venetian glass beads by stringing each bead on a piece of wire and then making a wrapped loop on each end. Add dangles to the loops created in Step 1. Alternate the mother-of-pearl flowers with the rectangular Venetian beads, connecting the loops with jump rings. Add dangles to the jump ring connections. Finish by adding a lobster clasp.

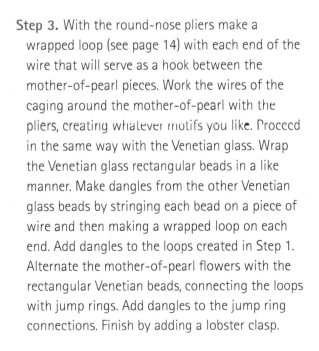

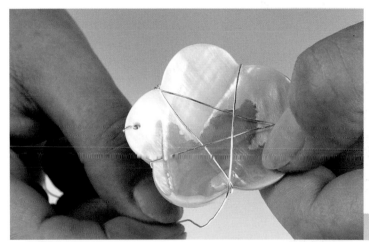

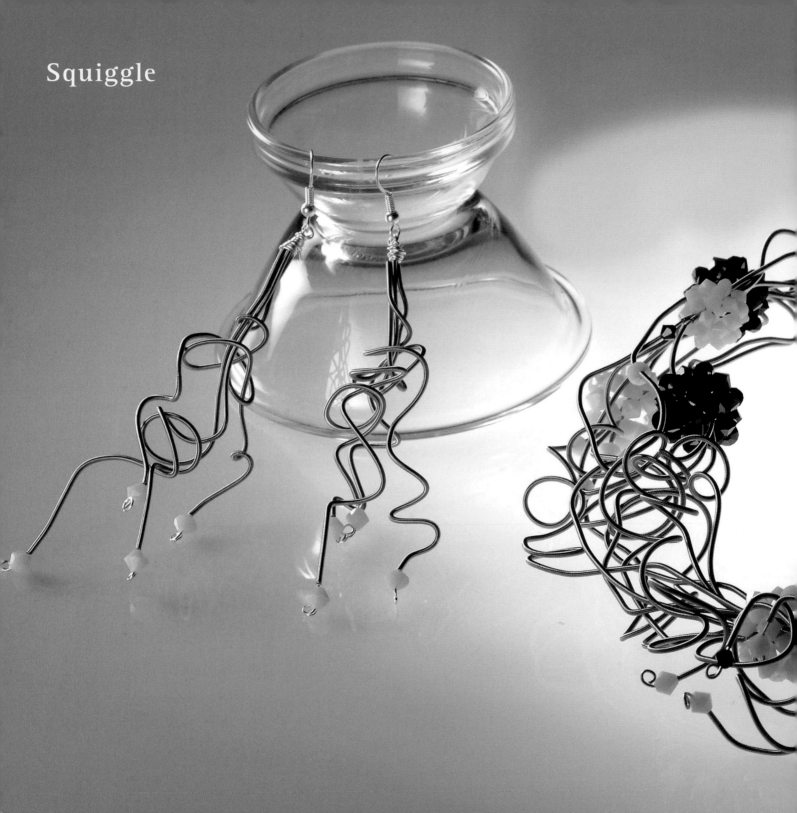

Squiggle

Materials
- 44 flexible 8" (20cm) wires
- 394" (1,000cm) length of 18-gauge silver wire
- 2 large knot cups
- 2 head pins
- 1 lobster clasp
- 1 soldered ring
- 210 crystals no larger than 5mm
- 70 crystals no larger than 4mm
- 24" (60cm) nylon thread

Tools
- Round-nose pliers
- Scissors

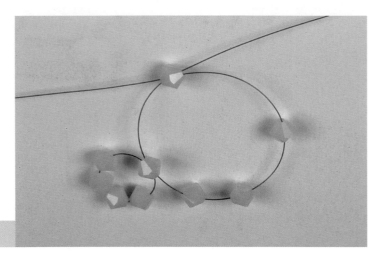

Step 1. Cut a 24" (60cm) piece of nylon thread and put 5 crystals on it. Cross on the last beaded crystal and bring the work to the center. Insert 3 crystals on one of the two ends, and put 1 crystal on the other end. Cross on the single crystal.

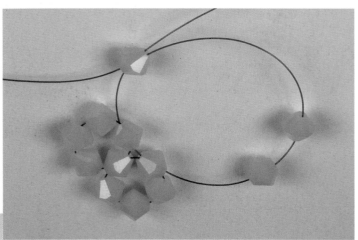

Step 2. On the inner thread that holds a crystal from the preceding curve, string 1 crystal, and on the other end string 2 crystals. Cross on the single crystal. To close it, take 1 crystal from the preceding curve and the opposite one, string 1 crystal on both threads, and cross on one of the 2 crystals.

Step 3. Take 1 crystal from the next flower, string 2 crystals on 1 thread and 1 crystal on the other, cross on the single crystal.

Step 4. To close the little ball, at the end of the second curve pass through 3 crystals, string 1 crystal, and make a surgeon's knot (see page 13).

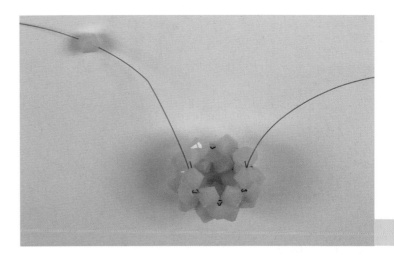

Step 5. Cut off the tightest part on the flexible wire. Then cut 10 pieces of flexible wire about 39" (1 m) long and on each piece place 4 pieces, spreading them apart at certain points with a crystal. Slide a ball of crystals on and bring it to the center, distribute the others on the two sides of the necklace.

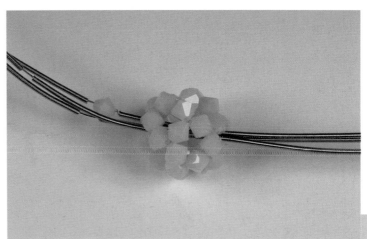

Step 6. On both sides twist the wires among themselves. Insert the head pin on the excess wire and make a loop. Then add a knot cup and a lobster clasp and form another loop. Repeat on the other side, inserting the soldered jump ring. Bend the wires in a pleasing arrangement to complete the necklace.

Crocheted
Bracelets

Materials

- 1 reel of 30-gauge silver wire
- 8 gray 12mm pearls
- 30 gray 8mm pearls
- 9 safety pins
- 1 flat, drilled 2.5cm mother-of-pearl piece
- 2 lobster clasps

Tools

- Size 3 crochet hook
- Flat-nose pliers
- Wire cutters

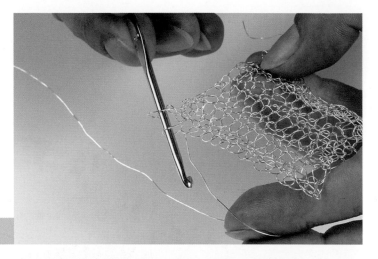

Step 1. For the crochet, make a base chain of desired length. Put the crochet hook through the chain of the next stitch and pull up a loop. Wrap the wire over the hook again and pull it through the loops on the hook. Repeat rows of these two steps until you obtain your desired width (shown here 6¹/₄" [16cm]).

Step 2. Position the mother-of-pearl piece on the crocheted base. Cut a piece of silver wire, string 1 pearl on it, and pass it back through the mother-of-pearl hole.

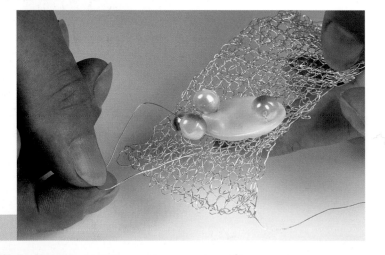

Step 3. Continue to add pearls with the wire ends. The pearls should be connected one by one. Create harmonious compositions. Join the wire on the back and hide the winding between the stitches. Add the lobster clasps to one end.

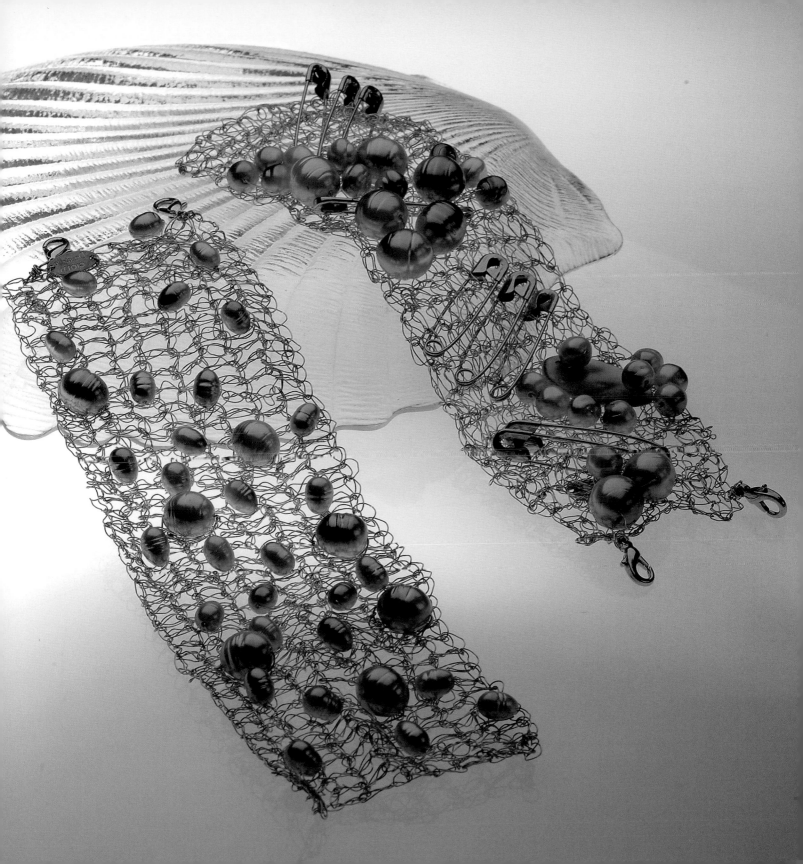

Wood and Buttons

Ethnic Motifs
in Wood

Materials
- 150 wooden 8–10mm
  beads in various shapes
- 10 wooden 16mm beads
- 157" (399cm) length of
  linen cord

Tools
- Scissors
- Tape measure

Step 1. To make the necklace on the preceding page, cut 4 pieces of linen cord 39" (1m) long. On the first, string the various-shaped small wooden beads for a length of 6" (15cm), on the second for a length of 8" (20cm), on the third 10" (25cm), on the fourth 12" (30cm). Group the 4 strings together and pass them through 3 or 4 of the 16mm wooden beads. Repeat the process on the other side, grouping them together.

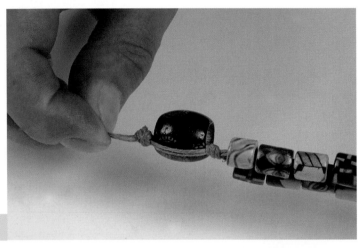

Step 2. On both sides divide the cords into two groups of 2, and on each group string small wooden beads until you reach your desired length. At the end of one of the two sides, create a knot and make a loop. On the other side, make a simple knot, and string a 16mm wooden bead where a few strings will pass through the hole and others on the outside. Make a second knot to secure.

To make the necklace on the facing page:

Step 3. To create the dangles that will make it unique, cut a piece of cord, and knot it around the group of cords. One strand will pass inside the wooden bead and the other on the outside. Finish with a surgeon's knot (see page 13).

TORCHON NECKLACE
This variation was made by tying together many strands threaded with wooden components.

Entwinement of Metal and Wood

Materials for the Bracelet

- 16 wooden 8, 10, and 16mm beads
- 1 lobster clasp
- 48" (122cm) length of 8-gauge silver wire

Tools for the Bracelet

- Flat-nose pliers
- Wire cutters

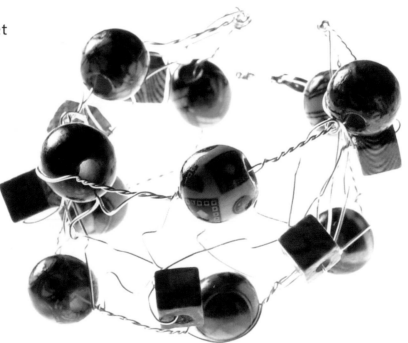

Materials for the Necklace

- 55 wooden 8, 10, and 16mm beads
- 394" (1,000cm) length of 18-gauge silver wire
- 1 lobster clasp

Tools for the Necklace

- Wire cutters
- Round-nose pliers

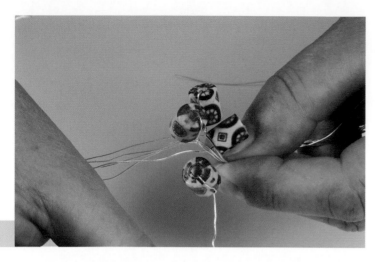

Step 1. Cut 6 pieces of silver wire about 39" (1m) long. On one piece, string a wooden bead, push it to the center of the wire, bend the wire toward the outside of the bead, and twist it at the base. Do this with the other wires as well.

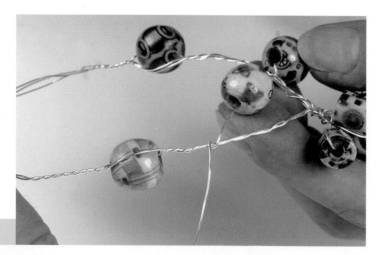

Step 2. To the right and to the left of the central figure you've just made, make a few twists with 2 or 3 of the wires. Divide the wires into groups of 2, twist each group for about 1" (2–3cm), string a bead on a wire, pass the other one behind, and continue with the twisting. Do this on both sides of the necklace.

Step 3. With a new piece of wire, after having stretched out the wires used for the groups in the work you have just done, connect them with coils of wire on which you have strung more beads. Continue working, using the photo on page 83 as a guide, creating entwining effects.

Step 4. If you run out of wire while working, join it with little twists near a bead and trim the excess. Start working again with a new piece of wire. To finish, both for the bracelet and for the necklace, make little zigzags with round-nose pliers so that you create movement on the wire.

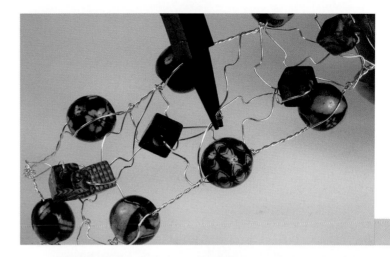

Step 5. On one of the two sides, even the wires and twist them among themselves about 1½" (4cm), bend the twist into a loop, and wrap it closed. You will have then formed the hook and eye clasp.

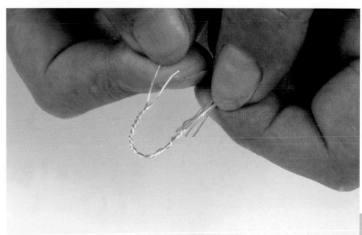

Step 6. On the other side, even and twist the wires among themselves for about 1½" (4cm), string the lobster clasp, join the wires so that they hold the lobster clasp, and wrap it closed. To make the bracelet, follow the directions given for the necklace, only reduce to obtain 19¾" (50cm) pieces of the silver wire.

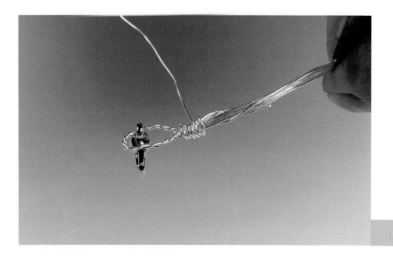

Buttons
and Chain

Materials for the Bracelet
- 8 mother-of-pearl 2.5cm flower-shaped buttons in various colors
- 16" (40cm) of small linked chain
- 2 lobster clasps
- 2 soldered rings
- 79" (200cm) length of 20-gauge silver wire

Tools for the Braclet
- Wire cutters

Materials for the Necklace
- 20" (50cm) of small linked chain
- 29 mother-of-pearl 1" (2.5cm) buttons in various shapes and colors
- 1 lobster clasp
- 1 soldered ring
- 157" (394cm) length of 20-gauge silver wire

Tools for the Necklace
- Wire cutters
- Round-nose pliers

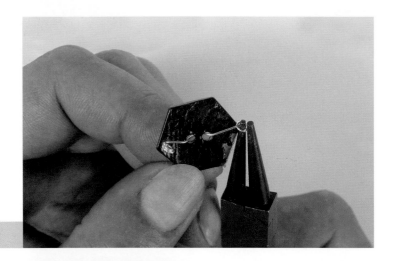

Necklace

Step 1. Cut a 4" (10cm) length of silver wire, pass an end through a buttonhole, and pass it through the other hole. Pull the wire tightly and cut the excess, leaving just enough for a small coil at each end. Make a small coil on both ends with the round-nose pliers (see page 19). Do all of the buttons this way except the ones you'll use for the pendants.

Step 2. Separate a length of 8 chain links. Open the last one and insert it in the coil you just made. Close the link.

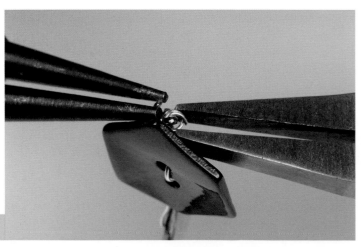

Step 3. Do the same thing on the other side, hooking a new button there. Continue connecting buttons and links of chain for the length of the choker.

1

2

3

Step 4. For the pendants, stack 2 buttons and link them with the silver wire, as described in Step 1. Take a piece of chain with 15 links and hook it to the two ends of one of the chain sections of the choker. Connect the pendant to the center ring. Repeat for the eight center sections of the choker.

Bracelet
Step 1. Cut 2 pieces of chain about 7–8" (18–20cm). Cut one 4" (10cm) piece of silver wire and insert it through both holes of the flower. Insert one of the two ends of silver wire through the center link of one of the two pieces of chain. With the round-nose pliers, make a ring and roll the wire two to three times to its base. Trim the excess wire.

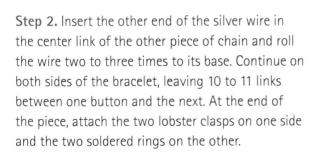

Step 2. Insert the other end of the silver wire in the center link of the other piece of chain and roll the wire two to three times to its base. Continue on both sides of the bracelet, leaving 10 to 11 links between one button and the next. At the end of the piece, attach the two lobster clasps on one side and the two soldered rings on the other.

Knotted
Buttons

Materials
- 60 mother-of-pearl 1" (2.5cm) buttons
- 120' (36m) of waxed gray or green cord

Tools
- Scissors
- Tape measure

Step 1. Cut 14 pieces of waxed cord 6½' (2m) long and one 8' (2.5m) long. Gather the cords together. Fold them over at one end and make a knot to create a loop for the closure. Make half hitches around the loop with the longest cord (see page 56). Make a second knot at 6" (15cm) away, a third at 8" (20cm) from the second, and a fourth 6" (15cm) from the previous one. String 4 large, round buttons and make a new knot that you'll use for a fastener. Cut a piece of cord 6" (15cm) in length, wrap it around the center of the bundle, and make two knots.

Step 2. Pass the ends of the cord through both holes of 1 button. Make a surgeon's knot (see page 13). Trim the ends even with the edges of the button. Continue adding buttons to cover the center of the necklace.

Step 3. For the pendants, cut 6 pieces of cord 12" (30cm) in length and string 2–3 buttons on. Knot the pendant to the base of the necklace, hiding the knot between the base buttons. End each pendant cord with a small knot.

BUTTONS AND METALLIC TUBULAR MESH RIBBON
In this variation the mother-of-pearl buttons
are strung on metallic tubular mesh ribbon,
creating unique color effects.

Blue drop strung on beading wire and, variation,
on two strands of metallic tubular mesh ribbon.

White drop strung on cords
closed with thread wraps.

Various Applications
for Teardrops

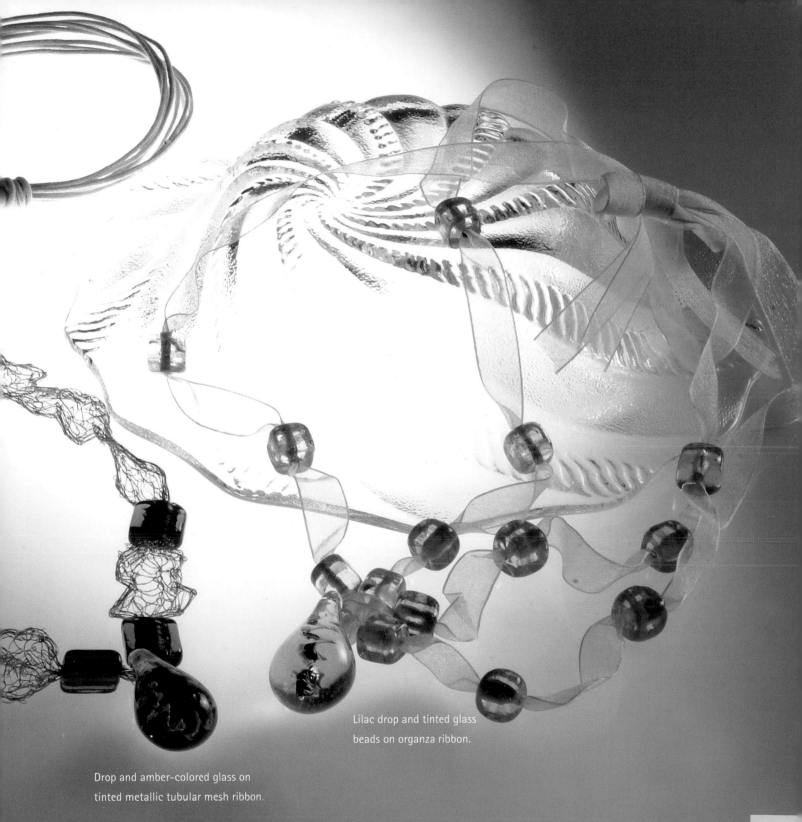

Lilac drop and tinted glass
beads on organza ribbon.

Drop and amber-colored glass on
tinted metallic tubular mesh ribbon.

Suppliers

Most of the materials for the projects in this book were created specifically according to Donatella's requirements. Suppliers Donatella used are as follows:

Donatella Ciotti's own haberdashery shop:

Merceria Donatella
Via Mascheroni 18
27100 Pavia
Italy
tel. / fax +39.0382.23675

Guarmet srl
Viale Col di Lana 14
20136 Milano
Italy
website: www.guarmet.it
e-mail: guarmet@guarmet.it
tel: +39.02.58104161
fax +39.02.89400296

The following specialty items seen in projects in this book can also be found at Fire Mountain Gems:

Czech pressed glass
Silk thread
Soldered rings
Mother-of-pearl figures,
    pendants, and beads
Flexible wire
Cotton waxed cord
Chain
Metallic tubular mesh ribbon

One Fire Mountain Way
Grants Pass, OR 97526-2373
(800) 355-2137
www.firemountaingems.com

Basic beading materials can be found at the following suppliers, organized by material:

Buttons:
JHB International*
(303) 751-8100
www.buttons.com

Pressed glass and general beading supplies:
Beadcats
PO Box 2840
Wilsonville, OR 97070-2840
(503) 625-2323
www.beadcats.com

Seed beads and general beading supplies:
Beadalon*
(866) 4-BEADALON
www.beadalon.com

Halcraft USA Inc.*
(212) 376-1580
www.halfcraft.com

Out on a Whim
121 E. Cotati Ave.
Cotati, CA 94931
(800) 232-3111
www.whimbeads.com

Rio Grande
7500 Bluewater Rd. NW
Albuquerque, NM 87121
(800) 545-6566
www.riogrande.com

Shipwreck Beads
8560 Commerce Place Dr. NE
Lacey, WA 98516
(800) 950-4232
www.shipwreckbeads.com

Stormcloud Trading Co.
725 Snelling Ave. N
St. Paul, MN 55104
(651) 645-0343
www.beadstorm.com

Thunderbird Supply Company
1907 W Historic Rte. 66
Gallup, NM 87301
(800) 545-7968
www.thunderbirdsupply.com

Semiprecious stones and general beading supplies:
Fire Mountain Gems
One Fire Mountain Way
Grants Pass, OR 97526-2373
(800) 355-2137
www.firemountaingems.com

Sequins and buttons:
Cartwright's Sequins &
    Vintage Buttons
11108 N. Hwy. 348
Mountainburg, AR 72946
(479) 369-2074
www.ccartwright.com

Specialty beads and findings:
Blue Moon Beads*
www.bluemoonbeads.com

Sterling silver charms and bracelets:
Charm Factory Inc.
PO Box 91625
Albuquerque, NM 87199
(866) 867-5266
www.charmfactory.com

Swarovski crystals and pearls:
Beyond Beadery
PO Box 460
Rollinsville, CO 80474
(800) 840-5548
www.beyondbeadery.com

Venetian glass and beads:
Bella Venetian Beads
1292 Rickert Drive, Suite 156
Naperville, IL 60540
(630) 305-8232
www.bellavenetianbeads.com

Lady From Venice
(310) 691-2871 (United States)
011 39 0415239784 (Italy)
www.ladyfromvenice.it

Luigi Cattelan
Fondamenta Vetrai, 115
30141 Murano-Venezia
Italy
041 736494
www.gomurano.com

*Wholesale or distributor only.

Index